Classic QUILTS

by The Keystone Quilters

D0568664

First Printing: 2005

Library of Congress Cataloging-in-Publication Data
Classic quilts / by the Keystone Quilters ;
[compiled by Christiane Meunier].
    p. cm.
  ISBN 1-885588-66-6 (pbk.)
1. Patchwork—Patterns. 2. Quilting—Patterns.
I. Meunier, Christiane. II. Keystone Quilters.
TT835.C5934 2005
746.46'041—dc22

2005010454

Design and Illustrations: Diane Albeck-Grick • **Photography:** Van Zandbergen Photography, Brackney, Pennsylvania

Our Mission Statement We publish quality quilting books that recognize, promote, and inspire self-expression.
We are dedicated to serving our customers with respect, kindness, and efficiency.

www.QuiltTownUSA.com

OHIO VALLEY MUSINGS
By Sara Madson
Page 4

THE
STRIPE
QUILT
By Kathy Kean
Page 10

A
SUGGESTION
OF BUNNIES
By Virginia Jones
Page 20

NIDS & GRIDS
By Maria Tamaoka
Page 18

MATERIALS

- 3/4 yard red print
- 8 1/4 yards white
- Fat eighth (11" x 18") pink print
- Fat eighth dark pink
- Fat eighth dark brown
- Fat quarter (18" x 22") brown check
- Scraps of brown, red, pink, and blue prints (mostly brown) in light to dark values, 7 yards total
- 1 yard blue print
- Scraps of brown and blue plaids and prints, 1 1/4 yards total
- 1 yard brown print for the binding
- 8 1/2 yards backing fabric
- 92" x 104" piece of batting

Ohio Valley Musings

CUTTING

Dimensions include a 1/4" seam allowance.

For the center square:
- Cut 1: 5 1/4" square, red print
- Cut 2: 3 1/4" squares, red print
- Cut 8: 2 7/8" squares, red print
- Cut 4: 2 7/8" x 5 1/4" rectangles, white
- Cut 2: 3 1/4" squares, white
- Cut 4: 2 7/8" squares, white
- Cut 2: 1" x 11" strips, pink print
- Cut 2: 1" x 10" strips, pink print

For the small Sawtooth Border:
- Cut 16: 2 3/8" squares, white
- Cut 8: 2 3/8" squares, red
- Cut 8: 2 3/8" squares, dark brown
- Cut 2: 2 3/4" x 18 1/2" strips, brown check
- Cut 2: 2 3/4" x 14" strips, brown check

For the Diamond in a Square Border:
- Cut 20: 2 5/8" squares, brown, red, and pink prints
- Cut 4: 3" squares, brown print, then cut them in half diagonally to yield 8 triangles
- Cut 12: 4 1/4" squares, white, then cut them in quarters diagonally to yield 48 triangles
- Cut 4: 2" squares, brown print
- Cut 32: 1 1/4" squares, red print
- Cut 16: 1 1/4" x 2" rectangles, white
- Cut 16: 1 1/4" squares, white

For the Double Sawtooth border:
- Cut 64: 2" x 4" rectangles, white
- Cut 128: 2" squares, red print
- Cut 4: 2 1/4" squares, brown print
- Cut 32: 1 3/8" squares, red print

- Cut 16: 1 3/8" x 2 1/4" rectangles, white
- Cut 16: 1 3/8" squares, white

For the small Flying Geese border:
- Cut 56: 2 3/4" x 5" rectangles, brown prints
- Cut 112: 2 3/4" squares, white
- Cut 4: 2 3/4" squares, brown prints
- Cut 32: 1 5/8" squares, red print
- Cut 16: 1 5/8" x 2 3/4" rectangles, white
- Cut 16: 1 5/8" squares, white

For the Hour Glass border:
- Cut 20: 5 1/4" squares, brown and pink prints, then cut them in quarters diagonally to yield 80 triangles
- Cut 2: 5 1/4" squares, white, then cut them in quarters diagonally to yield 8 triangles
- Cut 36: 3 3/8" squares, white

(continued on page 6)

Inspired by a quilt in the Virginia Quilt Museum, Sara Madson of Crowley, Texas, stitched *"Ohio Valley Musings"*, a title that honors her mother and grandmother who were born in the Ohio Valley in West Virginia. Sara's hand pieced and hand quilted work won ribbons at the Mid Atlantic Quilt Festival, New York Quilts, and Quilts=Art=Quilts.

(continued from page 4)

- Cut 4: 2 1/2" squares, brown prints
- Cut 32: 1 1/2" squares, red print
- Cut 16: 1 1/2" x 2 1/2" rectangles, white
- Cut 16: 1 1/2" squares, white

For the large Sawtooth border:
- Cut 32: 3 7/8" squares, blue print
- Cut 32: 3 7/8" square, white
- Cut 4: 2" squares, scraps brown print
- Cut 32: 1 1/4" squares, red print
- Cut 16: 1 1/4" x 2" rectangles, white
- Cut 16: 1 1/4" squares, white

For the Variable Star border:
(patterns on page 13)
- Cut 44: A, brown prints
- Cut 352: C, brown prints, in sets of 8
- Cut 176: B, white
- Cut 176: D, white
- Cut 80: E, white
- Cut 16: F, white

For the large Flying Geese border:
- Cut 112: 3" x 5 1/2" rectangles, assorted dark prints
- Cut 52: 3" squares, blue print
- Cut 172: 3" squares, assorted light and medium prints

For the Pinwheel border:
- Cut 48: 3 1/8" squares, assorted brown prints
- Cut 48: 3 1/8" squares, white
- Cut 11: 7 1/2" squares, white, then cut them in quarters diagonally to yield 44 large triangles
- Cut 4: 4" squares, white and cut them in half diagonally to yield 8 small triangles

For the small Sawtooth border:
- Cut 28: 4 3/4" squares, assorted brown prints
- Cut 28: 4 3/4" squares, white

For the Streak of Lightening border:

- Cut 32: 7 1/4" squares, assorted brown and blue plaids and prints, then cut them in quarters diagonally to yield 128 triangles
- Cut 125: 1 1/2" x 4 3/4" strips, white

Also:
- Cut 11: 2 1/2" x 42" strips, brown print for the binding

DIRECTIONS

For the Center:

1. Draw a diagonal line from corner to corner on the wrong side of each 2 7/8" white square.

2. Place a marked square on one corner of a 5 1/4" red print square, right sides together. Stitch on the drawn line, as shown.

3. Press the white square toward the corner, aligning the edges. Trim the seam allowance 1/4" beyond the stitching.

4. In the same manner, lay a marked square on each of the other corners, stitch on the marked line, press, and trim as before to make a large Square-in-a-square, as shown.

5. Draw a diagonal line on the wrong side of each 2 7/8" red print square.

6. Place a marked red square on one end of a 2 7/8" x 5 1/4" white rectangle. Stitch on the marked

line, press and trim as before.

7. In the same manner, stitch, press, and trim a marked square to the other end of the white rectangle to make a Flying Geese unit, as shown. Make 4. Set them aside.

8. Draw a diagonal line from corner to corner on the wrong side of each 3 1/4" white square.

9. Place a marked square on a 3 1/4" red print square, right sides together. Stitch 1/4" away from the drawn line on both sides, as shown. Make 2.

10. Cut the squares on the drawn lines to yield 4 small pieced squares.

11. Lay out the large Square-in-a-square, the 4 Flying Geese units, and the 4 small pieced squares, as shown.

12. Stitch them into rows and join the rows to make the center block. It should measure 10" square.

13. Stitch the 1" x 10" pink print strips to opposite sides of the center block.

14. Stitch the 1" x 11" pink print strips to the remaining sides of the center block. The unit should measure 11" square.

For the small Sawtooth border:

1. Draw a diagonal line from corner to corner on the wrong side of each 2 3/8" white square.

2. Place a marked square on a 2 3/8" dark brown square, right sides together. Stitch 1/4" away from the drawn line on both sides. Make 8 dark brown/white and 8 red/white. Cut the squares on the drawn lines to yield 32 pieced squares.

3. Lay out 4 brown pieced squares and 3 red pieced squares alternately, as shown. Stitch them into a row. Make 4.

4. Stitch 2 of the rows to opposite sides of the center square.

5. Referring to the photo for proper positioning, stitch the remaining red pieced squares to the ends of the remaining rows.

6. Stitch the rows to the remaining sides of the center square.

7. Stitch the 2 3/4" x 14" brown check strips to opposite sides of the center square.

8. Stitch the 2 3/4" x 18 1/2" brown check strips to the remaining sides of the center square. The unit should measure 18 1/2" square.

For the Diamond-in-a-Square border:

1. Lay out five 2 5/8" brown, red, and pink squares, 2 brown print triangles and 12 white triangles, as shown.

2. Stitch them into diagonal rows and join the rows to make a border. Make 4. Set them aside.

3. Draw a diagonal line from corner to corner on the wrong side of each 1 1/4" red print square.

4. Place a marked square on one end of a 1 1/4" x 2" white rectangle, right sides together. Stitch on the drawn line. Press and trim as before.

5. In the same manner, stitch a marked square on the other end of the white rectangle. Press and trim as before to complete a Flying Geese unit. Make 16.

6. Lay out four 1 1/4" white squares, 4 Flying Geese units, and a 2" brown print square, as shown.

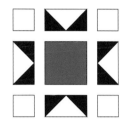

7. Stitch the pieces into rows and join the rows to make a Variable Star block. Make 4.

8. Stitch Diamond-in-a-Square borders to 2 opposite sides of the center square.

9. Stitch a Variable Star block to each end of the remaining borders.

10. Stitch them to the remaining sides of the center square, as shown. The unit should measure 24 1/2" square.

For the Double Sawtooth border:

1. Draw a diagonal line from corner to corner on the wrong side of each 2" red print square.

2. Place a marked red square on one end of a 2" x 4" white rectangle, right sides together. Stitch on the drawn line, as shown.

3. Press the red square toward the corner, aligning the edges. Trim the seam allowance 1/4" beyond the stitching.

4. In the same manner, lay a marked red square on the opposite end of the white rectangle, as shown. Stitch on the marked line. Press and trim as before. Make 64.

5. Lay out 16 pieced rectangles, as shown, and stitch them together to make a border. Make 4. Set them aside.

6. Make 16 Flying Geese units, as before, using the 1 3/8" red print squares and the 1 3/8" x 2 1/4" white rectangles.

7. Lay out four 1 3/8" white squares, four Flying Geese units, and a 2 1/4" brown print square. Join them to make a Variable Star block, as before. Make 4.

8. Stitch Double Sawtooth borders to 2 opposite sides of the center square.

9. Stitch a Variable Star block to each end of the remaining Double Sawtooth borders.

10. Stitch the borders to the remaining sides of the center square, as shown. The unit should measure 31 1/2" square.

For the small Flying Geese border:

1. Draw a diagonal line from corner to corner on the wrong side of each 2 3/4" white square.

2. Make 56 Flying Geese units as described before using the marked 2 3/4" white squares and the 2 3/4" x 5" brown print rectangles.

3. Lay out 14 Flying Geese units and stitch them together to make a border, as shown. Make 4. Set them aside.

4. Make 4 Variable Star blocks, as described before, using the 2 3/4" brown print squares, the 1 5/8" red print squares, the 1 5/8" x 2 3/4" white rectangles, and the 1 5/8" white squares.

5. Stitch Flying Geese borders to two opposite sides of the quilt. NOTE: *You may have to adjust the borders slightly to fit the quilt.*

6. Stitch a Variable Star block to each end of the remaining Flying Geese borders.

7. Stitch them to the remaining sides of the quilt. The quilt should measure 40 1/2" square.

For the Hour Glass border:

1. Lay out nine 3 3/8" white squares, 2 white triangles, and 20 brown and pink triangles, as shown.

2. Stitch the squares and triangles in diagonal rows and join the rows to make an Hour Glass border. Make 4.

3. Make 4 Variable Star blocks, as before, using the 2 1/2" brown print squares, 1 1/2" red print squares, 1 1/2" x 2 1/2" white rectangles, and 1 1/2" white squares.

4. Stitch Hour Glass borders to two opposite sides of the quilt. Adjust the borders if necessary.

5. Stitch a Variable Star block to each end of the remaining Hour Glass borders.

6. Stitch them to the remaining sides of the quilt. The quilt should measure 48 1/2" square.

For the Large Sawtooth border:

1. Draw a diagonal line from corner to corner on the wrong side of each 3 7/8" white square.

2. Place a marked square on a 3 7/8" blue print square, right sides together. Stitch 1/4" away from the drawn line on both sides. Make 32.

3. Cut the squares on the drawn lines to yield 64 pieced squares.

4. Lay out 16 pieced squares and join them to make a border, as shown. Make 4.

5. Make 4 Variable Star blocks, as before, using the 2" brown print squares, 1 1/4" red print squares, 1 1/4" x 2" white rectangles, and 1 1/4" white squares.

6. Stitch Sawtooth borders to 2 opposite sides of the quilt.

7. Stitch a Variable Star block to each end of the remaining Sawtooth borders.

8. Stitch them to the remaining sides of the quilt. The quilt should measure 54 1/2" square.

For the Variable Star border:

1. Stitch 2 brown print C's to a white B. Make 4.

2. Stitch B/C units to opposite sides of a brown print A.

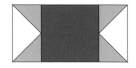

3. Stitch white D's to the remaining B/C units. Stitch the strips to the remaining sides of the A to make a Star block. Make 44.

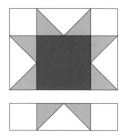

4. Lay out 10 Star blocks, 18 white E's, and 4 white F's. Stitch the units into diagonal rows and join the rows to make a border. Make 2.

5. Stitch the borders to opposite sides of the quilt.

6. In the same manner, lay out 12 Star blocks, 22 white E's, and 4 white F's. Stitch them into diagonal rows and join the rows. Stitch the borders to the remaining sides of the quilt. Make 2.

7. The quilt should measure 65 1/2" square.

For the large Flying Geese border:

1. Draw a diagonal line from corner to corner on the wrong side of each 3" blue print square and each 3" light and medium square.

2. Make 26 Flying Geese units as described before, using the marked blue print squares and twenty-six 3" x 5 1/2" dark rectangles. Make 86 Flying Geese units using the marked light and medium squares and the remaining dark rectangles.

3. Lay out 26 blue print Flying Geese units and stitch them together to make a border. Sew the border to one side of the quilt.

4. Lay out 26 Flying Geese units and stitch them together to make a border. Stitch it to the opposite side of the quilt.

5. Join 30 flying Geese units to make a border. Make 2. Stitch the borders to the remaining sides of the quilt. The quilt should measure 75 1/2" square.

For the Pinwheel border:

1. Draw a diagonal line from corner to corner on the wrong side of each 3 1/8" white square.

2. Make 96 pieced squares as before, using the marked white squares and the 3 1/8" assorted brown print squares.

3. Lay out 4 pieced squares in either arrangement, as shown. Join them to make a Pinwheel block. Make 24.

4. Lay out 12 Pinwheel blocks, 22 large white triangles, and 4 small white triangles. Sew the pieces into diagonal rows and join the rows to make a border. Make 2.

5. Sew the borders to opposite sides

of the quilt. The quilt should measure 75 1/2" x 88".

For the small Sawtooth border:

1. Draw a diagonal line from corner to corner on the wrong side of each 4 3/4" white square. Draw horizontal and vertical lines through the centers.

2. Place a marked square on a 4 3/4" brown print square, right sides together. Sew 1/4" away from the diagonal lines on both sides.

(continued on page 13)

QUILT SIZE: 71 1/2" x 89 1/2"
BLOCK SIZE: 16 1/2" square

MATERIALS

- 1/4 yard each of 12 dark prints for the stars
- 1/4 yard each of 12 light prints for the background
- 1/2 yard each of 12 stripe fabrics
- 2/3 yard blue stripe for the block centers and cornerstones
- 3/4 yard green print
- 1 1/4 yards brown print
- Stripe fabric with 16 motifs each at least 3" square
- 7/8 yard dark print for the binding
- 7 1/2 yards backing fabric
- 80" x 100" piece of batting

CUTTING

Dimensions include a 1/4" seam allowance.

From each dark print:
- Cut 4: 3 1/4" squares
- Cut 32: 1 7/8" squares

From each light print:
- Cut 32: 1 7/8" squares
- Cut 16: 1 7/8" x 3 1/4" rectangles

From each stripe:
- Cut 20: 1 5/8" x 13" strips
  NOTE: *Separate the strips into 4 piles of 3 and 4 piles of 2.*

Also:
- Cut 3: 1 5/8" x 13" strips, one stripe
- Cut 2: 1 5/8" x 13" strips, contrasting stripe
- Cut 16: 6" squares, blue stripe
- Cut 31: 2" x 17" strips, brown print
- Cut 20: 2" squares, green print
- Cut 7: 2 1/2" x 42" strips, green print

- Cut 16: 3 1/2" squares, stripe fabric, centering a motif in each square
- Cut 9: 2 1/2" x 42" strips, dark print, for the binding

DIRECTIONS

For each set of 4 Star blocks:

1. Draw a diagonal line from corner to corner on the wrong side of sixteen matching 1 7/8" light print squares and 32 matching dark print squares.

2. Place marked light squares on opposite corners of a 3 1/4" dark print square. Sew on the drawn lines.

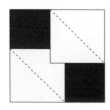

3. Press the squares toward the cor-

ners, aligning the edges. Trim the seam allowances to 1/4".

4. Place marked light print squares on the remaining corners of the dark print square. Sew, press, and trim as before to complete a Square-in-a-square. Make 4.

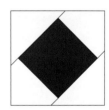

5. Place a marked dark print square on one end of a 1 7/8" x 3 1/4" light print rectangle. Sew on the drawn line. Press and trim, as before.

6. Place a marked dark square on the opposite end of the rectangle.

(continued on page 12)

*"**The Stripe Quilt**" was made by Kathy Kean of Kathy's Kreations in Charleston, South Carolina. Kathy says, "I was playing with stripes one day and this is the result. It reminds me of the antique quilts that used men's shirting." This cozy quilt won a blue ribbon in the South Carolina Coastal County Fair.*

(continued from page 10)

Sew, press, and trim to complete a Star point unit. Make 16.

7. Lay out a Square-in-a-square, 4 Star point units, and four 1 7/8" light print squares. Sew them into rows and join the rows to complete a Star block. Make 4.

8. In the same manner, make 11 more sets of 4 Star blocks. Set them aside.

9. Join three 1 5/8" x 13" stripe strips alternately with two 1 5/8" x 13" contrasting stripe strips along their length. Make 2 matching panels.

10. In the same manner, make 23 more sets of matching panels and one single panel.

11. Measure the width of a panel. Trim an equal amount from both edges if necessary to make the panel 6" wide. Repeat for the remaining striped panels.

12. Cut two 6" sections from each pieced panel.

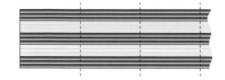

13. Press the edges of each 3" motif square 1/4" toward the wrong side. Center a square on each 6" blue stripe square and appliqué them in place. Set 4 aside for the cornerstones.

14. Lay out 4 matching stripe squares, 4 matching Star blocks, and one 6" blue stripe square. Sew the squares into rows and join the rows to make a block. Make 12.

ASSEMBLY

1. Referring to the photo on page 11, lay out the blocks in 4 rows of 3. Place the 2" x 17" brown print strips between the blocks and on the outside of the layout. Place the 2" green print squares between the brown strips.

2. Sew the squares and horizontal strips into rows. Sew the blocks and vertical strips into rows. Join the rows.

3. Sew the 2 1/2" x 42" green print strips together, end to end, to make a long pieced strip.

4. Measure the length of the quilt. Cut two lengths from the pieced strip each equal to that measurement and sew them to the long sides of the quilt.

5. Measure the width of the quilt. Cut two lengths from the pieced strip each equal to that measurement and sew them to the remaining sides of the quilt.

6. Sew 14 stripe squares together, alternating the direction of the stripes, to make a long border. Refer to the photo as necessary. Make 2.

7. Measure the length of the quilt. If necessary, adjust the long borders to make them the same length as the quilt.

8. Sew 11 stripe squares together to make a short border. Adjust them, if necessary. Make 2.

9. Sew the blue stripe cornerstones to the ends of the short borders.

10. Sew the long borders to the long sides of the quilt.

11. Sew the short borders to the remaining sides of the quilt.

12. Finish the quilt as described in the *General Directions*, using the 2 1/2" x 42" dark print strips for the binding.

(continued from page 9)

3. Cut the squares on the drawn lines to yield 224 pieced squares. You will use 218.

4. Join 58 pieced squares to make a long border. Make 2.

5. Sew the borders to the long sides of the quilt, placing the white triangles against the quilt.

6. Join 51 pieced squares, turning the last one, as shown. Make 2.

7. Sew the borders to the short sides of the quilt, placing the brown triangles against the quilt. The quilt should measure 78 1/2" x 90 1/2".

For the Streak of Lightening border:

1. Sew dark triangles and 1 1/2" x 4 3/4" white strips together, as shown.

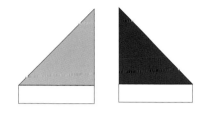

2. Sew 28 units together to make a border.

3. Measure the width of the quilt. Trim the border to that measurement. Sew it to the top of the quilt.

4. In the same manner, sew 33 units together to make a border. Make 2.

5. Measure the length of the quilt. Trim the borders to that measurement. Sew them to the sides of the quilt.

6. Sew 31 units together to make a border.

7. Measure the width of the quilt. Trim the border to that measurement and sew it to the bottom of the quilt.

8. Finish the quilt as described in the *General Directions*, using the 2 1/2" x 42" brown print strips for the binding.

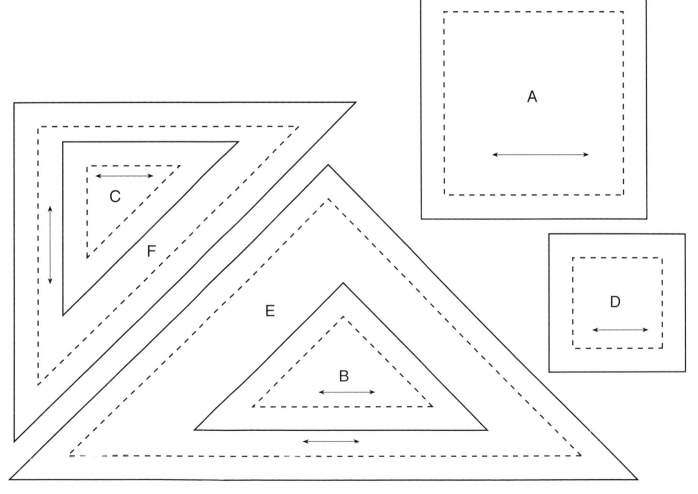

MATERIALS

- 1 1/4 yards rust print
- 28 fat quarters (18" x 22") assorted prints
- 3 yards beige print
- 3 1/2 yards yellow print for the inner border and binding
- 8 3/4 yards of backing fabric
- 93" x 102" piece of batting
- Tracing paper

CUTTING

Appliqué patterns (page 32) are full size and do not include a turn-under allowance. Make a template for each of the pieces. Trace around the templates on the right side of the fabric and add a 1/8" to 3/16" turn-under allowance when cutting the fabric pieces out. All other dimensions, including the piecing patterns on page 17, include a 1/4" seam allowance.

For each of 56 House blocks:

- Cut 3: 1 1/2" x 3 1/2" strips, first print, for the house side
- Cut 2: 1 1/2" x 5 1/2" strips, first print
- Cut 2: 1 1/2" x 4 1/2" strips, second print, for the house front
- Cut 1: 1 1/2" x 3 1/2" strip, second print
- Cut 1: A, second print
- Cut 1: B, third print

From the rust print:

- Cut 56: 1 1/2" x 4 1/2" strips
- Cut 112: 1 1/2" x 3 1/2" strips
- Cut 184: 1 1/2" squares
- Cut 2: 5" squares

From the beige print:

- Cut 127: 1 1/2" x 8 1/2" strips, for the sashing
- Cut 56: 1 1/2" x 3 1/2" strips
- Cut 112: 1 1/2" x 2" strips
- Cut 56: C
- Cut 56: CR

From the yellow print:

- Cut 4: 9 1/2" x 83" strips, for the inner border
- Cut 10: 2 1/2" x 42" strips, for the binding
- Cut 2: 5" squares

For the outer border:

- Cut 174: 1 1/2" x 2" strips, beige print
- Cut 88: 1 1/2" x 2 3/4" strips, beige print
- Cut 84: 1 1/2" x 3 3/4" strips, assorted prints
- Cut 174: 1 1/2" x 2 1/4" strips, assorted prints
- Cut 88: 1 1/2" squares, assorted prints

Also:

- Cut 38: D, assorted prints
- Cut 38: E, assorted prints
- Cut 76: F, assorted green prints
- Cut 38: 3/4" x 4 3/4" bias strips, assorted green prints, for the stems

DIRECTIONS

For each House block:

1. Stitch three 1 1/2" x 3 1/2" first print strips and two 1 1/2" x 3 1/2" rust print strips together, as shown.

2. Stitch 1 1/2" x 5 1/2" first print strips to the top and bottom of the pieced section, as shown, to make a window unit. Set it aside.

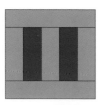

(continued on page 16)

14

*Claire Theophanis of Friendsville, Pennsylvania, crafted "**Tu-lips All Around.**" The unusual fabrics in Claire's quilt, which she discovered at an area quilt show, are originally from the Netherlands. Claire, an avid bird watcher, and her husband Chris live in a round log house nestled in the wooded hills of Northern Pennsylvania. Claire is always eager to share information about her feathered friends and about quilting.*

(continued from page 14)

3. Stitch a 1 1/2" x 4 1/2" rust print strip between two 1 1/2" x 4 1/2" second print strips, as shown.

4. Stitch a 1 1/2" x 3 1/2" second print strip to the top of the pieced section, as shown, to make a door unit.

5. Stitch the door unit to the left side of the window unit. Set it aside.

6. Lay out the A, B C, and CR as shown. Stitch them together.

7. Stitch two 1 1/2" x 2" beige print strips, two 1 1/2" rust print squares, and a 1 1/2" x 3 1/2" beige print strip together, as shown.

8. Stitch the two units together to make a roof unit.

9. Stitch the roof unit to the top of the window and door unit, to complete a House Block. Make 56.

ASSEMBLY

1. Referring to the quilt photo, lay out the blocks, 1 1/2" x 8 1/2" beige print sashing strips, and the remaining 1 1/2" rust print squares.

2. Stitch them into rows and join the rows.

3. Measure the length of the quilt. Trim two 9 1/2" x 83" yellow print strips to that measurement.

4. Stitch them to the long sides of the quilt.

5. Measure the width of the quilt, including the borders. Trim the remaining 9 1/2" x 83" yellow print strips to that measurement.

6. Stitch them to the remaining sides of the quilt.

For the outer border:

1. Draw diagonal lines from corner to corner on the wrong side of each 5" yellow print square. Draw horizontal and vertical lines through the centers.

2. Place a marked square on a 5" rust print square, right sides together. Stitch 1/4" away from both sides of the diagonal lines, as shown. Make 2.

3. Cut the squares on the drawn lines to yield 16 pieced squares. Press the seam allowance toward the rust print fabric.

4. Lay out 4 squares, as shown, and stitch them together to make a Pinwheel block. Make 4. Set them aside.

5. Join a short edge of a 1 1/2" x 2" beige print strip to a 1 1/2" x 2 1/4" print strip. Make 174.

6. Stitch a 1 1/2" print square to a 1 1/2" x 2 3/4" beige print strip. Make 88.

7. Stitch 2 pieced strips from the first group and one from the second group together to make a border unit, as shown. Make 86.

8. Stitch 20 border units and twenty 1 1/2" x 3 3/4" assorted print strips together alternately, to make a short border. Stitch one of each pieced strip to one end of the border, maintaining the pattern. Make 2.

9. Stitch twenty-two 1 1/2" x 3 3/4" assorted print strips and 23 border units together alternately to make a long border. Make 2.

10. Stitch the long borders to the sides of the quilt.

11. Stitch a Pinwheel block to each end of the short borders. Stitch the borders to the remaining sides of the quilt.

12. Trace the appliqué tulips on a sheet of tracing paper. Using the

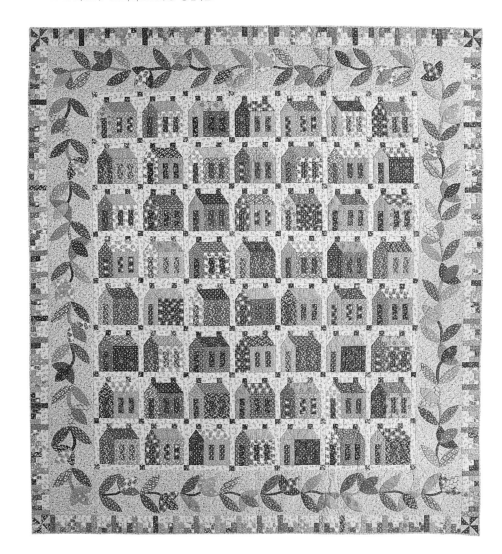

quilt photo for placement, lightly trace the tulip design from the tracing paper onto the inner border.

13. Use the tip of your needle to turn under the allowance as you appliqué each piece in place. Use the drawn line for placement of the appliqué pieces. There is no need to turn under the allowance where pieces overlap. Appliqué the pieces in the following order: 3/4" x 4 3/4" green print bias strips as stems, tulips (D and E), and the leaves (F).

14. Finish the quilt as described in the *General Directions*, using the 2 1/2" x 42" yellow print strips for the binding.

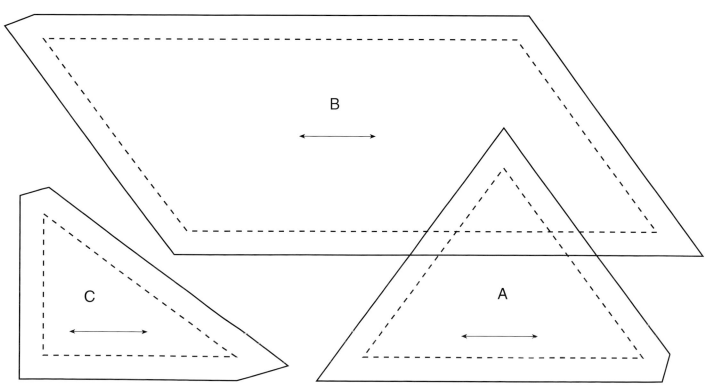

QUILT SIZE: 64" x 90"

BLOCK SIZE: 10 3/4" square

MATERIALS

- 24 prints each at least 12" square
- 2 1/4 yards light print for the block grids
- 3/4 yard red print for the blocks and cornerstones
- 2 1/4 yards gold print for the sashing and binding
- 1 1/2 yards gold print for the border
- 5 1/2 yards backing fabric
- 68" x 94" piece of batting

CUTTING

Dimensions include a 1/4" seam allowance.

For each of 24 blocks:

- Cut 4: 2 5/8" x 12" dark strips

Also:

- Cut 16: 2 5/8" x 24" lengthwise strips, light print
- Cut 10: 1 1/4" x 24" lengthwise strips, light print
- Cut 72: 1 1/4" x 12" lengthwise strips, light print
- Cut 20: 1 1/4" x 24" lengthwise strips, red print
- Cut 58: 2 3/4" x 11 1/4" strips, gold print, for the sashing
- Cut 9: 2 1/2" x 42" strips, gold print, for the binding
- Cut 8: 5 1/2" x 42" crosswise strips, gold print, for the border

DIRECTIONS

1. Sew four 2 5/8" x 24" light print strips and three 1 1/4" x 24" red print strips together alternately to make a panel. Make 4. Press the seam allowances toward the red print.

2. Cut eighteen 1 1/4" sections from each panel. Set them aside.

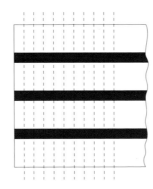

For each block:

1. Sew four 2 5/8" x 12" print strips and three 1 1/4" x 12" light print strips together alternately to make a panel. Press the seam allowances toward the print strips.

2. Cut four 2 5/8" sections from the panel.

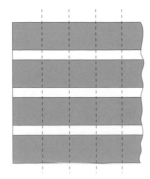

3. Lay out the 4 sections and 3 sections from Step 2. Sew them together to make a block. Make 24. Set them aside.

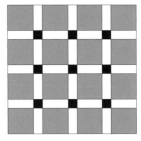

For the Nine Patch Cornerstones:

1. Sew two 1 1/4" x 24" light print strips to a 1 1/4" x 24" red print strip to make a panel. Make 4.

2. Cut seventy 1 1/4" sections from the panels.

3. Sew two 1 1/4" x 24" red print strips to a 1 1/4" x 24" light print strip to make a panel. Make 2.

4. Cut thirty-five 1 1/4" sections from the panels.

18

(continued on page 23)

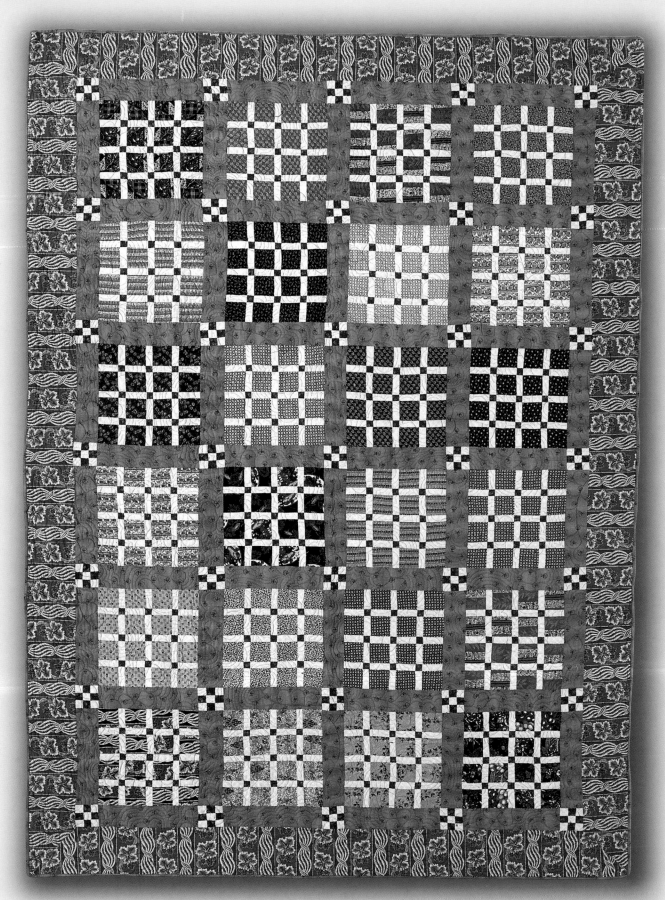

*Quilts which are easy in construction but use great fabric, that's what Maria Tamaoka of Croton-on-Hudson, New York, favors. She designed "**Nids & Grids**" to use reproduction prints by Mary Koval from Windham Fabrics. Maria also loves Japanese Daiwabo Taupe fabric which she distributes in her shop Pinwheels, in Croton-on-Hudson, New York. The quilt was quilted by Debby Brown.*

19

QUILT SIZE: 55" x 69"

BLOCK SIZE: 5" square and 4" square

MATERIALS

- Assorted medium to dark prints, each at least 8" square
- 4 yards white
- 3 1/2 yards backing fabric
- 59" x 73" piece of batting

CUTTING

Dimensions include a 1/4" seam allowance. Cut the lengthwise white border strips before cutting the smaller pieces from that fabric.

For each of 35 Block A's:

- Cut 2: 3 3/8" squares, one dark print, then cut them in half diagonally to yield 4 triangles
- Cut 2: 3 3/4" squares, medium print

For each of 34 Block B's:

- Cut 2: 2 7/8" squares, one dark or medium print

From the white:

- Cut 2: 1 3/4" x 63" lengthwise strips
- Cut 2: 1 3/4" x 52" lengthwise strips
- Cut 70: 3 3/4" squares
- Cut 68: 2 7/8" squares
- Cut 24: 5 1/2" squares
- Cut 2: 4 1/2" squares, then cut them in half diagonally to yield 4 corner triangles
- Cut 5: 8 3/8" squares, then cut them in quarters diagonally to yield 20 setting triangles
- Cut 17: 7" squares, then cut

them in quarters diagonally to yield 68 border setting triangles

- Cut 4: 2" x 12" strips
- Cut 15: 5 3/4" squares
- Cut 4: 2 1/2" squares

Also:

- Cut 15: 5 3/4" squares, assorted medium to dark prints
- Cut 100: 1 1/4"-wide straight-grain strips, assorted medium dark prints, each 5" to 7" long, for borders
- Cut 60: 2 1/2"-wide straight-grain strips, assorted medium dark prints, each 6" to 8" long, for the binding

DIRECTIONS

For Block A's:

1. Draw diagonal lines from corner to corner on the wrong side of two 3 3/4" white squares.

2. Place a marked white square on a 3 3/4" medium print square, right sides together.

3. Stitch 1/4" away from both sides of one diagonal line. Make 2.

4. Cut the squares on the drawn lines to yield 8 pieced triangles. Half will have the print on the right and half will have the print on the left. You will use only the triangles with the print on the right, as shown. Press the seam allowances open.

5. Stitch a pieced triangle to a dark print triangle to make a pieced square, as shown. Make 4.

6. Stitch the pieced squares together, as shown, to complete Block A. Make 35. Set them aside.

For Block B's:

1. Draw a diagonal line from corner to corner on the wrong side of two 2 7/8" white squares.

2. Place a marked white square on a

(continued on page 22)

"A Suggestion of Bunnies" was the first quilt Virginia Jones of Taunton, Massachusetts, quilted by hand. She used it as a sampler of quilting motifs, with each setting square and triangle a different design. Mixed in with the many traditional motifs are some unique designs, including a pair of adult rabbits and a litter of bunnies.

(continued from page 20)

2 7/8" dark or medium print square, right sides together. Stitch 1/4" away from the drawn line on both sides. Make 2.

3. Cut the squares on the drawn lines to yield 4 pieced squares. Press the seam allowances toward the dark side.

4. Stitch the pieced squares together, as shown, to complete Block B. Make 34. Set them aside.

For the Sawtooth Border:

1. Draw diagonal lines from corner to corner on the wrong side of each 5 3/4" white square. Draw horizontal and vertical lines through the center.

2. Place a marked white square on a 5 3/4" medium to dark print square, right sides together. Stitch 1/4" away from the diagonal lines on both sides. Make 15.

3. Cut the squares on the drawn lines to yield 120 pieced squares. Press the seam allowances toward the dark side. You will use 118.

ASSEMBLY

1. Lay out the Block A's on-point in 7 rows of 5, with 5 1/2" white

squares between the blocks, white setting triangles along the edges and white corner triangles in the corners.

2. Stitch the blocks, squares and triangles into diagonal rows and join the rows.

3. Place 2 of the 1 1/4" wide medium to dark print strips, right sides together, at right angles to each other, as shown. Stitch a diagonal seam. Trim 1/4" from the seam.

4. Continue to stitch the 1 1/4"-wide print strips together in the same manner to form a pieced strip at least 420" long.

5. Cut two 50" long strips from the pieced strip. Stitch them to the long sides of the quilt.

6. Cut two 37 1/2" long strips from the pieced strip. Stitch them to the remaining sides of the quilt. Set aside the remainder of the pieced strip.

7. Stitch white border triangles to opposite sides of a Block B to form a border unit, as shown. Make 30.

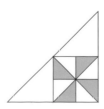

8. Stitch white border triangles to adjoining sides of a Block B to form a border corner unit. Make 4.

9. Stitch 9 border units together with a border corner unit to complete a long border. Make 2.

10. Center and stitch these borders to the long sides of the quilt, starting and stopping 1/4" from the raw edges.

11. In the same manner, stitch 6 border units together with a border corner unit.

12. Stitch a 2" x 12" white strip to each end and trim, as shown, to complete a short border. Make 2.

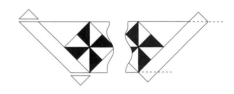

13. Center and stitch the short borders to the remaining sides of the quilt in the same manner. Miter each corner, referring to the mitering section in the *General Directions* as needed. NOTE: *You may need to trim the width of the white strips at the end of the short borders to make them fit properly.*

14. Cut two 63"-long strips and two 52"-long strips from the long pieced strip.

15. Stitch each of them to a 1 3/4"-wide white strip of the same length, along their lengths, to make borders.

16. Stitch the 2 longer borders to the long sides of the quilt, and then stitch the 2 shorter borders to the remaining sides of the quilt.

17. Stitch 26 pieced squares together, as shown, to make Sawtooth

border strips. Make 2.

18. Stitch the Sawtooth border strips to the short sides of the quilt.

19. In the same manner, stitch 33 pieced squares together. Make 2.

20. Stitch a 2 1/2" white square to each end.

21. Stitch them to the long sides of the quilt. NOTE: *You may need to trim the white squares by approximately 1/4" each, reducing the length to make these borders fit accurately.*

22. Join the 2 1/2"-wide medium to dark print strips with diagonal seams (see step 3) to form a long strip at least 270" long.

23. Finish the quilt as described in the *General Directions*, using the assorted 2 1/2"-wide strips for the binding. Stitch the binding strips together with diagonal seams.

NIDS & GRIDS

(continued from page 18)

5. Join 3 sections, alternating them as shown, to make a Nine Patch Cornerstone. Make 35.

ASSEMBLY

1. Sew 5 Cornerstones and four 2 3/4" x 11 1/4" gold print strips together alternately to make a sashing strip. Make 7.

2. Lay out the blocks in 6 rows of

4. Place the remaining 2 3/4" x 11 1/4" gold print strips between the blocks and at the beginning and end of each horizontal row.

3. Sew the blocks and strips into rows. Join the rows and sashing strips.

4. Sew the 5 1/2" x 42" gold print border strips together, end to end, taking care to match the design.

5. Measure the length of the quilt. Cut 2 lengths from the border strip, each equal to that measurement. Sew

them to the sides of the quilt.

6. Measure the width of the quilt, including the borders. Cut 2 lengths from the border strip, each equal to that measurement. Sew them to the top and bottom of the quilt.

7. Finish the quilt as described in the *General Directions*, using the 2 1/2" x 42" gold print strips for the binding.

QUILT SIZE: 75 1/2" square
BLOCK SIZE: 9" square

MATERIALS

- 1 1/4 yards red print
- 1 1/4 yards brown print
- 5/8 yard purple print
- 1 1/2 yards muslin
- 1 1/4 yards tan print
- 1 yard beige print for the sashing
- 2 1/4 yards floral for the outer border
- 4 1/2 yards backing fabric
- 80" square of batting

CUTTING

Dimensions include a 1/4" seam allowance.

- Cut 8: 2" x 42" strips, red print
- Cut 14: 8" squares, red print
- Cut 9: 1 1/2" squares, red print
- Cut 8: 2 1/2" x 42" strips, brown print, for the binding
- Cut 7: 8" squares, brown print
- Cut 8: 1 1/2" squares, brown print
- Cut 7: 8" squares, purple print
- Cut 8: 1 1/2" squares, purple print
- Cut 28: 8" squares, muslin
- Cut 108: 3 1/2" squares, tan print
- Cut 24: 1 1/2" squares, tan print
- Cut 84: 1 1/2" x 9 1/2" strips, beige print
- Cut 4: 6 1/4" x 78" strips, floral

DIRECTIONS

1. Draw diagonal lines from corner to corner on the wrong side of each 8" muslin square. Draw horizontal and vertical lines through the centers.

2. Place a marked square on an 8"

red print square, right sides together. Stitch 1/4" away from the diagonal lines on both sides. Make 14.

3. Cut the squares on the drawn lines to yield 112 pieced squares. You will use 108. Press the seam allowances toward the red print.

4. Trim each pieced square to 3 1/2".

5. In the same manner, make 56 purple pieced squares and 56 brown pieced squares using the 8" purple and brown print squares and the remaining 8" muslin squares. You will use 54 of each.

6. Lay out 3 red pieced squares, 3 brown pieced squares, and three 3 1/2" tan print squares. Stitch them into rows and join the rows to complete a block. Make 18.

7. Lay out 3 red pieced squares, 3 purple pieced squares, and three 3 1/2" tan print squares. Stitch them into rows and join the rows to complete a block. Make 18.

ASSEMBLY

1. Lay out the blocks in 6 rows of 6. Place the 1 1/2" x 9 1/2" beige print sashing strips between the blocks and on the outside of the layout. Place the 1 1/2" tan, red, brown, and purple print squares between the sashing strips, matching the squares with the adjacent blocks.

2. Stitch the horizontal sashing strips and 1 1/2" squares into rows.

3. Stitch the blocks and vertical sashing strips into rows.

4. Join the rows.

(continued on page 30)

*A beautiful floral gives the perfect finishing touch to **"Cherry Vanilla Swirl."** Chris Gingrich of Littleton, Colorado, says she likes to search for "fun fabrics with lots of movement." Chris has only been quilting for 4 years, having been introduced to it at a retreat where she lent her cooking skills. The professional quilting was done by J. Renee Howell of Skyline Studios in Centennial, Colorado.*

Square Dance

MATERIALS

- Assorted red, blue, and tan prints totaling at least 5 yards
- 3/4 yard navy print for the binding
- 4 yards backing fabric
- 67" x 76" piece of batting

CUTTING

Dimensions include a 1/4" seam allowance.

For each of 22 large-center blocks:
- Cut 1: 6 1/2" square, first print
- Cut 2: 2" x 9 1/2" strips, second print
- Cut 2: 2" x 6 1/2" strips, second print

For each of 34 small-center blocks:
- Cut 1: 3 1/2" square, first print
- Cut 2: 2" x 6 1/2" strips, second print
- Cut 2: 2" x 3 1/2" strips, second print
- Cut 2: 2" x 9 1/2" strips, third print
- Cut 2: 2" x 6 1/2" strips, third print

Also:
- Cut 8: 2 1/2" x 42" strips, navy print, for the binding

DIRECTIONS

For each large-center block:
Press all seam allowances toward the outside of the block.

1. Sew the 2" x 6 1/2" second print strips to opposite sides of the 6 1/2" first print square.

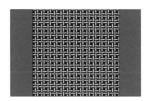

2. Sew the 2" x 9 1/2" second print strips to the remaining sides to complete a block. Make 22.

For each small-center block:
3. Sew the 2" x 3 1/2" second print strips to opposite sides of the 3 1/2" first print square. Sew the 2" x 6 1/2" second print strips to the remaining sides.

4. Sew 2" x 6 1/2" third print strips to opposite sides of the square and 2" x 9 1/2" third print strips to the remaining sides. Make 34.

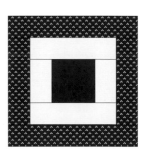

ASSEMBLY

1. Lay out the blocks in 8 rows of 7. Stitch them into rows and join the rows.

2. Stitch them into rows and join the rows.

3. Finish the quilt as described in the *General Directions*, using the 2 1/2" x 42" navy print strips for the binding.

Debra Feece of Montrose, Pennsylvania, wanted to make a quick quilt to use up some of her fabric. What could be easier than squares and strips? This scrappy design could be made in plaids, batiks, flannels, homespuns or any other favorite fabric. Make "**Square Dance**" according to the directions or make only 49 blocks for a 63"–square throw-size quilt.

MATERIALS

- Assorted prints, each at least 4 1/2" x 7 1/2", and totaling at least 5 yards
- 2 yards medium blue print
- 2 3/4 yards dark blue print
- 6 yards backing fabric
- 69" x 89" piece of batting

Dashing Through the Past

CUTTING

Dimensions include a 1/4" seam allowance.

For each of 111 Churn Dash blocks:

- Cut 2: 3" squares, one dark print
- Cut 4: 1 1/2" squares, same dark print
- Cut 2: 3" squares, one light print
- Cut 5: 1 1/2" squares, same light print

Also:

- Cut 14: 13" squares, dark blue print
- Cut 14: 13" squares, medium blue print
- Cut 8: 2 1/2" x 42" strips, dark blue print, for the binding

DIRECTIONS

For each Churn Dash block:

1. Draw a diagonal line from corner to corner on the wrong side of each 3" light print square.

2. Place a marked square on a 3" dark print square, right sides togeth-er. Sew 1/4" away from the drawn line on both sides. Make 2.

3. Cut the squares on the drawn lines to yield 4 pieced squares. Press the seam allowances open. Trim the pieced squares to 2 1/2" square.

4. Sew a 1 1/2" dark square to a 1 1/2" light square. Press the seam allow-ances toward the dark square. Make 4.

5. Lay out the pieced squares, 2-square units, and remaining 1 1/2" light square. Sew them into rows and join the rows to complete the block. Make 111.

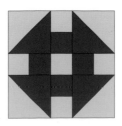

For the Hourglass blocks:

1. Draw diagonal lines from corner to corner on the wrong side of each 13" medium blue print square. Draw horizontal and vertical lines through the centers.

2. Place a marked square on a 13" dark blue print square, right sides together. Sew 1/4" away from the diagonal lines on both sides. Make 14.

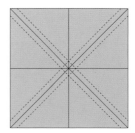

3. Cut the squares on the lines to yield 112 pieced squares. You will use 110.

4. Press the seam allowances toward the dark blue.

5. Draw a diagonal line, perpen-dicular to the seamline, on the wrong side of each of 55 pieced squares.

(continued on page 30)

*Civil War and Smithsonian
Reproduction fabrics were used
by Judy Madden of Ketchikan, Alaska,
to make "**Dashing Through the Past.**"
Each Churn Dash block has two fabrics used
only in that block. This quilt is a companion
to another quilt of reproduction fabrics Judy
made with Nine Patch and Hourglass blocks.*

(continued from page 28)

6. Place a marked pieced square on an unmarked pieced square, right sides together, placing the dark sides against the light sides. Sew 1/4" away from the drawn line on both sides. Make 55.

7. Cut the squares on the drawn lines to yield 110 Hourglass blocks. Press the seam allowances open. Trim each block to 5 1/2" square.

ASSEMBLY

1. Referring to the photo, lay out the blocks in 17 rows of 13. Sew the blocks into rows and join the rows.

2. Finish the quilt as described in the *General Directions*, using the 2 1/2" x 42" dark blue strips for the binding.

CHERRY VANILLA SWIRL

(continued from page 24)

5. Stitch two 2" x 42" red print strips together end to end to make a border strip. Make 4.

6. Center and stitch a red print border strip to a 6 1/4" x 78" floral strip to make a border. Make 4.

7. Center and stitch the borders to the sides of the quilt. Start, stop, and backstitch at the 1/4" seamline.

8. Miter the corners in the following way: With the quilt top right side down, lay one border over the other.

Using a pencil, draw a straight line at a 45° angle from the inner to the outer corners.

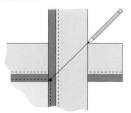

9. Reverse the positions of the borders and mark another corner-to-corner line. With the borders right sides together and the marked seamlines carefully matched, stitch from the inner seamline to the outer corner, backstitching at each end. Open the mitered seam to make sure it lies flat, then trim the excess fabric and press. Repeat for the remaining corners.

10. Finish the quilt as described in the *General Directions*, using the 2 1/2" x 42" brown print strips for the binding.

GENERAL DIRECTIONS

About the patterns

Read through the pattern directions before cutting fabric. Yardage requirements are based on fabric with a useable width of 42". Pattern directions are given in step-by-step order. If you are sending your quilt to a professional machine quilter, consult the quilter regarding the necessary batting and backing size for your quilt.

Fabrics

I suggest using 100% cotton. Wash fabric in warm water with mild detergent. Do not use fabric softener. Dry fabric on a warm-to-hot setting. Press with a hot dry iron to remove any wrinkles.

Templates

Template patterns are full size and unless otherwise noted, include a 1/4" seam allowance. The solid line is the cutting line; the dashed line is the stitching line. Templates for hand piecing do not include a seam allowance.

Piecing

For machine piecing, sew 12 stitches per inch, exactly 1/4" from the edge of the fabric. To make accurate piecing easier, mark the throat plate with a piece of tape 1/4" to the right of the point where the needle pierces the fabric.

Appliqué

Appliqué pieces can be stitched by hand or machine. To hand appliqué, baste or pin the pieces to the background in stitching order. Turn the edges under with your needle as you appliqué the pieces in place. Do not turn under or stitch edges that will be overlapped by other pieces. Finish the edges of fusible appliqué pieces with a blanket stitch made either by hand or machine.

To machine appliqué, baste pieces in place close to the edges. Then stitch over the basting with a short, wide satin stitch using a piece of tear-away stabilizer under the background fabric. You can also turn the edges of appliqué pieces under as for needleturn appliqué, and stitch them in place with a blind-hem stitch.

Pressing

Press with a dry iron. Press seam allowances toward the darker of the two pieces whenever possible. Otherwise, trim away 1/16" from the darker seam allowance to prevent it from shadowing through. Press abutting seams in opposite directions. Press all blocks, sashings, and borders before assembling the quilt top.

Mitered Borders

Measure the length of the quilt top and add 2 times the border width plus 2". Cut border strips this measurement. Match the center of the quilt top with the center of the border strip and pin to the corners. Stitch— beginning, ending, and backstitching each seamline 1/4" from the edge of the quilt top. After all borders have been attached, miter one corner at a time. With the quilt top right side down, lay one border over the other. Draw a straight line at a 45° angle from the inner to the outer corners.

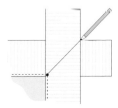

Reverse the position of the borders and mark another corner-to-corner line. With the borders right sides together and the marked seamlines carefully matched, stitch from the inner to the outer corner, backstitching at each end. Open the mitered seam to make sure it lies flat, then trim excess fabric and press.

FINISHING YOUR QUILT

Binding

Cut the binding strips with the grain for straight-edge quilts. Binding for quilts with curved edges must be cut on the bias. To make 1/2" finished binding, cut 2 1/2"-wide strips. Sew strips together with diagonal seams; trim and press seam allowance open.

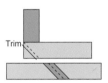

Fold the strip in half lengthwise, wrong side in, and press. Position the strip on the right side of the quilt top, aligning the raw edges of the binding with the edge of the quilt top. Leaving 6" of the binding strip free and beginning a few inches from one corner, stitch the binding to the quilt with a 1/4" seam allowance measuring from the raw edge of the quilt top. When you reach a corner, stop stitching 1/4" from the edge of the quilt top and backstitch. Clip the threads and remove the quilt from the machine. Fold the binding up and away from the quilt, forming a 45° angle, as shown.

Keeping the angled fold secure, fold the binding back down. This fold should be even with the edge of the quilt top. Begin stitching at the fold.

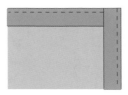

Continue stitching around the quilt in this manner to within 6" of the starting point. To finish, fold both strips back along the edge of the quilt so that the folded edges meet about 3" from both lines of the stitching and the binding lies flat on the quilt. Finger press to crease

the folds. Measure the width of the folded binding. Cut the strips that distance beyond the folds. (In this case 1 1/4" beyond the folds.)

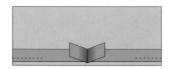

Open both strips and place the ends at right angles to each other, right sides together. Fold the bulk of the quilt out of your way. Join the strips with a diagonal seam as shown.

Trim the seam allowance to 1/4" and press it open. Refold the strip wrong side in. Place the binding flat against the quilt, and finish stitching it to the quilt. Trim excess batting and backing so that the binding edge will be filled with batting when you fold the binding to the back of the quilt. Blindstitch the binding to the back, covering the seamline.

Remove visible markings. Make a label that includes your name, the date the quilt was completed, and any other pertinent information, and stitch it to the back of your quilt.

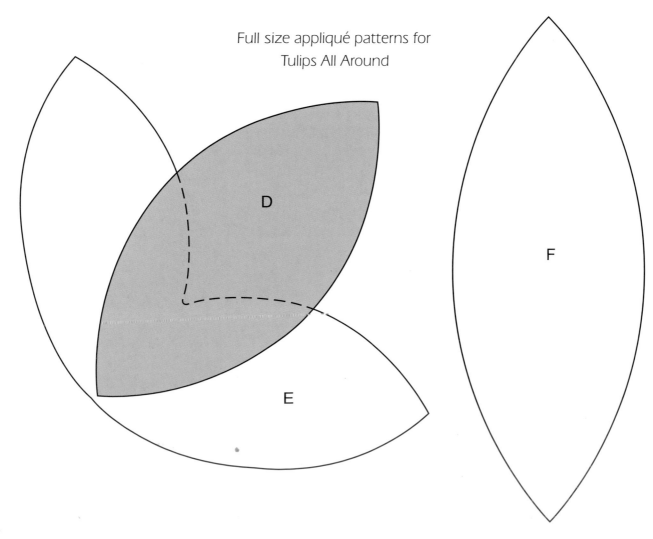

Full size appliqué patterns for
Tulips All Around